Smoothies

& BEYOND

Tori Ritchie

PHOTOGRAPHS
Maren Caruso

weldonowen

contents

blending like a pro

For years I used a dime-store blender. People told me about the superpowers of pro-blenders, but I refused to listen. I didn't need one, I thought. Smoothies came out fine in my old model, the one with buttons that indicate "grind-chop-purée"—although it didn't really seem to do any of those things. The things I made in it were a little grainy perhaps, a little chalky maybe, but overall okay.

Then I got a Vitamix® Professional Series™ blender and, like other modern wonders—Greek yogurt, smartphones—I can't imagine life without it. Everything I make in it is creamier and silkier than if had used a food mill and strained it through the finest sieve, as I was trained to do in culinary school. I can throw unpeeled carrots and apples or a market basket of produce into the container and whirl them up without losing any nutrients, so it's a fresh and pure way to eat. Better still, I can make much more than smoothies. Hot and cold soups, sauces and pestos, vegetable dips, salad dressings—I make them all in the Vitamix machine. As a result, my life is easier and healthier.

When I sat down (or stood up, actually, at the counter where my Vitamix machine resides) to create the recipes for this book, I realized there's another aspect to pro-blending that isn't talked about often: It's an amazing way to create decadent desserts like rich mousses, creamy puddings, and warm sauces. I can even pro-blend ice creams and sorbets without having to get out my ice cream machine.

I use my Vitamix machine all day, not just in the morning, so the chapters in this book reflect that. There are recipes for breakfast, lunch, dinner, and dessert, and many of them can be eaten as snacks. The dishes in this book can be served every day, on weekends, for parties, and for holidays. Most are healthy, but some are indulgent. They are meant to give you a broad taste of what you can do with your pro-blender, so start here to master the basics before taking off in your own direction. The best recipe may be hiding in your refrigerator, so rummage around in there and see what you can come up with.

how pro-blending works

Pro-blending is pretty simple: The blender's powerful engine makes the blades turn so fast that they process foods in a matter of seconds. You can blend any number of piping hot or freezing cold items in the same machine: It can crush ice and frozen ingredients into thick, cold concoctions in under a minute. However, if you let the machine run longer, about 5–6 minutes, the blades will create enough friction to heat liquid until steaming hot. There is no cooling element or heating coil within the pro-blender; the cooling or heating is all caused by the friction of the blades.

Pro-blenders are renowned for making smoothies and nut milks, but they are also great for juices, purées, dips, butters, spreads, hot and cold soups, sweet and savory sauces, dressings, batters, creams, foams, and frozen desserts. You can also grind cereals, grains, and coffee and even make dough, preferably with the Dry Grains container (see page 10).

When you use a pro-blender, you control what goes into your food. You can use organic whole foods such as fruits, vegetables, nuts, grains, and seeds and get all the fiber, vitamins, and minerals they have to offer. You can sweeten things with sugar alternatives like maple syrup, honey, stevia, or agave, or use other ingredients, such as dates, cinnamon, and nutmeg instead of sweetener. On the savory side, you can blend in citrus zests and spices to amp up flavor so you need less salt. All this adds up to a healthy, wholesome way to prepare food. You put in only what you want, you make the texture as chunky or smooth as you like, and the result is as fresh and pure as you choose.

Pro-blending is also a great way to clean out your refrigerator. You'd be amazed how good the fruits and vegetables in your produce drawer taste when blended into a Perfect Green Smoothie (page 25) or as a Salad in a Glass (page 48).

THE JOYS OF PRO-BLENDING

- A pro-blender is really several appliances in one: blender, food processor, ice cream machine, electric beaters, and stove (for heating soups and sauces).

- Using a pro-blender cuts down on prep time. You don't have to get out bowls and whisks and ladles and sieves: Just roughly chop the ingredients, layer them in the blender container, and you're good to go.

- When using a pro-blender, there is no need to strain puréed mixtures to help improve the texture (unless you want the consistency of extracted juice), so you get maximum nutrients from the food.

- A pro-blender is so easy to clean, it actually cleans itself: Just fill the container halfway with warm water, add one or two drops of dish soap, whirl it clean, and rinse well.

A pro-blender's powerful engine turns the blades so fast, they process foods in a matter of seconds. Purées made in a pro-blender come out more creamy and silky than mixtures strained through a fine-mesh sieve.

getting to know your pro-blender

You can read the technical information in your machine's instruction manual (and you most certainly should), where you'll learn about the machine's basic elements. In a Vitamix® Professional Series™ blender there are five elements: the powerful engine (housed in the base), the control panel, the container, the lid (with removable plug), and the tamper. Different models offer different versions of these elements. You can find out more online as well as compare models, register your machine to take advantage of the warranty benefits, and buy additional parts or replace old ones. Following are a few things you should know before you start blending with your Vitamix machine:

the control panel

The panel design varies from machine to machine, but there is always a power switch and a speed-control dial. Professional-series models may also offer a hi-low switch, a pulse switch, or pre-programed settings. With these programs, all you have to do is choose the appropriate function and turn on the machine. The machine then does the work and stops itself when the recipe is complete.

the container

Depending on the model you select, the size of the blender container varies. The main difference is capacity. Measurements are marked on the outside of the container in ounces, cups, and milliliters. Some people prefer models with a low-profile container, so the machine will fit on the counter under an upper kitchen cabinet.

The standard container that comes with the pro-blender has a "wet" blade that pulls food *down* to blend it for maximum smoothness. This is the container you will use for almost everything you make, including the recipes in this book. A second container with a "dry" blade—which forces food *up* into the container to keep it from clumping—can be purchased separately. It doesn't process liquids well, but is great for grinding flour, grains, and coffee, and for kneading dough. The recipes in this book were developed specifically for use with the standard blender container.

the tamper

Unlike regular blenders or food processors, a pro-blender is designed to work continuously: You generally don't have to stop the motor, open the lid, and scrape down the sides, as you do with those other machines. For preparing thick ingredients and frozen concoctions in a Vitamix machine, a sturdy tamper helps push the food into the blades and keep air pockets from forming. The tamper is always used with the lid in place and is custom-designed so it will not hit the blades, even as you move it around. Thus, it's important to use only the tamper that comes with your specific machine when blending with the tamper.

Reminder: The tamper is designed so that it will never touch the blender blades. Be sure to use only the tamper that comes with your pro-blender model.

pre-programmed settings

Some Vitamix® models and other pro-blenders come with icons on the control panel that represent pre-programmed settings. If you don't have these on your machine, below are the comparable times and speeds to use in recipes that call for presets:

- **SMOOTHIE SETTING** Start at variable speed 1, then gradually increase to the machine's highest speed and run for 45–60 seconds.

- **PURÉE SETTING** Start at variable speed 1, then gradually increase to the machine's highest speed and run for about 1 minute.

- **FROZEN DESSERT SETTING** Start at variable speed 1, then gradually increase to the machine's highest speed and run for about 45 seconds.

- **HOT SOUP SETTING** Start at variable speed 1, then gradually increase to the machine's highest speed and run for 5–6 minutes.

- **CLEANING SETTING** Start at variable speed 1, then gradually increase to the machine's highest speed and run for 30–60 seconds.

Reminder: Always set the variable speed dial back to 1 after blending. That way the machine will be at the right speed next time you start it.

Puréeing, dry chopping, wet chopping, and pulsing can all be done with a pro-blender to achieve an array of diverse textures.

working with a pro-blender

Many associate these powerful machines with soups and smoothies for good reason: The results are fantastic. But a pro-blender does more than purée. It also makes quick work of chopping and grating raw ingredients, whether it's carrots and onions for a stir-fry, cheese to add to a sauce, or cabbage to use in a slaw. What's important to know is there are two ways that the blender can chop: the dry method and the wet method.

dry chopping

Use this method when a random chop is fine, for example, with firm vegetables such as carrots, nuts, or cheese that will be incorporated into a larger recipe. Put chunks of the food in the container or drop them through the lid plug opening with the blades running on a low variable speed. This will take only a few seconds and the results will vary in size and shape. For a more precise chop, use the wet chop method.

wet chopping

Use this method for slicing cabbage and other vegetables for salads (see Vietnamese-Style Vegetable Slaw, page 53), potatoes for hash browns, or any time you need a more uniform chop. Put large chunks of the food in the container and add enough water so that the food floats above the blades (this helps pull it down into the blades for a consistent cut). The amazing thing is how quickly this happens: Just a few pulses and food is shredded. Drain the food well and use as directed.

When cutting up fruits and vegetables that are going to be puréed in the pro-blender, pre-cut them with a knife. You don't have to worry about being precise—just chop things into 2- or 3-inch (5- or 7.5-cm) chunks. In general, cut long vegetables like carrots, celery, cucumbers, and green onions into thirds. If the food has a tender skin, like an apple or a peach, you don't have to peel it first. The pro-blender works so well, you won't even know the peel is in there, but you get the extra nutrition and fiber that comes from it.

pulsing

Use this method when you want a partially smooth consistency with some texture remaining. Select the desired variable speed and then turn the machine on and off using the pulse switch, repeating until the desired consistency is reached.

cleaning up

Possibly the most underrated feature of a pro-blender is that it cleans itself. Follow the instructions on page 8 or run the Cleaning Program on your Vitamix® machine (see page 11) if your model has one. Remember to put the lid on *tightly* (I once left it loose and had soapy water all over my counter). Do not put the container or lid in the dishwasher, which can damage them.

Reminder: As with all electric appliances, always read the instruction manual for your pro-blender before using it the first time. You can also seek out helpful online videos and websites devoted to pro-blending.

tips and tricks for pro-blending

You can be a bit of a mad scientist with your pro-blender, trying combinations that appeal to you until you get the flavors just right. That's how I discovered my Perfect Green Smoothie (page 25). I also love to wet chop in my Vitamix® machine: Now that I know how quickly I can shred cabbage for slaw, I make this and other chopped dishes much more often. And did I mention desserts? Thanks to my Vitamix® machine, the Warm White Chocolate–Cream (page 91) may be the best thing I've ever made with just two ingredients.

I encourage you to start with the recipes in this book, then experiment with your own creations. In the meantime, here are some of the things I've learned along the way to make using my Vitamix® Professional Series™ blender go smoothly.

- It's essential to put the ingredients into the container in the order called for in the recipe: liquids first, softer foods next, firmer foods on top, and any ice or frozen foods last. The heavier ingredients work to push the others down into the blades, which is essential to achieving the best texture.

- The higher the blender speed you use, the finer the texture will be. You can vary the texture by removing the cap in the lid and adding ingredients in stages through the lid plug opening; the first ingredients added will be completely puréed, the last ingredients added will be more finely chopped and lend texture to the mixture.

- When making chunky sauces, like tomato salsa, pulse the ingredients carefully; it happens faster than what you might be used to with a regular blender or food processor.

- Frozen desserts come out with the texture of soft serve ice cream. For a firmer texture, transfer frozen desserts to freezer containers and freeze them for a few hours. If they become too firm, set out the containers at room temperature for a few minutes or microwave for a few seconds before scooping.

- Soups and sauces will emerge steaming hot when using the soup function; if you want the liquid even hotter, pour it into a saucepan and heat it further on the stove top.

- Pre-cooking certain ingredients is important. For soups, you need to cook the aromatics— onions, leeks, shallots, and garlic—in a frying pan. For some custards, preheat the milk or cream in a saucepan or microwave it.

- The color of traditional dishes may be lighter in color than you expected, thanks to the aeration caused by the machine's powerful blades.

All the recipes in this book were developed using a Vitamix® Professional Series™ 750. The recipes will also work in other pro-blenders, but be sure to read the instruction manuals for your model first.

making smoothies with a pro-blender

Many people use the pro-blender to make healthy fruit or vegetable smoothie for a quick and nutrient-rich breakfast, snack, or other meal. Blend your favorite combination of fruits and/or vegetables along with milk, nut milk, or water. To make your smoothie even more nutritious, add in one or more of the following ingredients to a recipe yielding 16 fl oz (500 ml) before you add the ice cubes (turn to pages 22–27 for ideas). For supersmooth results, put the liquid into the container first, then add soft fruits, then harder or denser fruits, then put the ice on top to push everything down into the blades for even blending. You can substitute frozen fruit for ice, which makes a supercold and thick drink. For great texture, keep frozen bananas on hand to add to the smoothie instead of raw bananas.

3 tablespoons whole or chopped nuts or nut butter: try almonds, walnuts, cashews, hazelnuts; peanut butter, almond butter or other nut butter

1 tablespoon healthy oil such as coconut oil or flaxseed or omega oil

1 tablespoon fiber-rich seeds or coarse meal such as flax seeds or meal, chia seeds, wheat germ, or bran

1 scoop whey
protein powder

1 tablespoon healthy
sweetener such as honey,
maple syrup, or agave
nectar; or 1 teaspoon
granulated stevia;
or 2 pitted dates

breakfast

nut milk

You can make all kinds of fresh nut milks in a Vitamix® machine, but the two most versatile are almond and cashew milks. For the almond milk, soak the nuts overnight and let the mixture stand before straining; drink it as is or sweeten it to taste. For the cashew milk, you don't need to soak or strain the nuts, so you can whip up a batch on the spot. Blend dairy-free nut milks into smoothies, pour onto cereal or into coffee or tea, or drink them as a quick gulp of protein anytime.

To make the almond milk, put the almonds in a bowl and cover with cold water. Refrigerate overnight (the nuts will swell and soften). Drain the nuts and put them in the blender container. Add 3 cups (24 fl oz/750 ml) cold water. Put the lid on securely, turn the dial to variable 1, and start the machine. Increase the speed to the highest setting and blend for 1 minute. Stop the machine and let the mixture stand for 10–15 minutes to infuse the flavors. Pour the mixture through a cheesecloth-lined strainer into a jar, carafe, or bottle. If desired, stir in the maple syrup, vanilla, and sea salt. Use right away, or cover and refrigerate for up to 5 days.

To make the cashew milk, put the cashews in the blender container. Add 3 cups (24 fl oz/750 ml) cold water. Put the lid on securely, turn the dial to variable 1, and start the machine. Increase the speed to the highest setting and blend for 1 minute. Stop the machine. Pour the cashew milk into a measuring cup or other container and use right away, or cover and refrigerate for up to 5 days.

FOR THE ALMOND MILK

1 cup (5½ oz/170 g) raw almonds

3 cups (24 fl oz/750 ml) cold water, plus water to soak nuts

2 teaspoons maple syrup, preferably grade B (optional)

1½ teaspoons vanilla extract (optional)

Pinch of sea salt (optional)

FOR THE CASHEW MILK

1 cup (5½ oz/170 g) raw cashews

3 cups (24 fl oz/750 ml) cold water

Makes 3½ cups (28 fl oz/875 ml)

all-purpose fruit smoothie

1 cup (8 fl oz/250 ml) nut milk (page 21), regular milk, soy milk, orange juice, or water

¼ cup (1¼ oz/35 g) slivered almonds

1 ripe banana, broken into chunks

1 scoop whey protein powder (see Note; optional)

2 tablespoons honey, maple syrup, or agave syrup

1 cup (4 oz/125 g) frozen or fresh strawberries, raspberries, or blueberries

½ cup (4 oz/125 g) ice cubes (see Note)

OPTIONAL ADD-INS

Roughly chopped, peeled fresh or frozen mango, pear, or peach

½ cup (4 oz/125 g) plain yogurt

1 tablespoon flax meal, chia seeds, flax oil, coconut oil, or omega-oil blend

2 pitted medjool dates (omit the sweetener if using dates)

Makes about 16 fl oz (500 ml); 1 or 2 servings

This healthy drink gives you what you need to start the day: protein, carbohydrates, vitamins, minerals, and fiber. It's also portable, so you can sip it on the go. Protein powder is available in health food stores and many supermarkets, and it comes with its own scoop. You can add in or substitute many kinds of soft, ripe fruits for the berries.

Pour the liquid of choice into the blender container. Add the almonds, banana, protein powder (if using), honey or other sweetener, berries, and any optional add-ins. Put the ice on top. Put the lid on securely, turn the dial to the smoothie setting (or set the variable speed dial to 1), and start the machine. If using the smoothie setting, process until the machine turns itself off. If using the dial, increase the speed to the highest setting and run for 45 seconds, or until completely smooth.

Pour the smoothie into 1 or 2 glasses and serve right away.

Note: If you are using fresh instead of frozen fruit, increase the amount of ice cubes to 1 cup (8 oz/250 g).

perfect green smoothie

There may be endless green smoothies out there, but this one is fresh, vibrant, light, and clean. The mint is essential so don't skip it. You can vary the components endlessly, but a few key options are suggested here. I like either kale or spinach for the greens, but you can also use romaine lettuce or purchased mixed greens.

Pour the water into the blender container. Add the cucumber, grapes, pineapple, greens, and mint. Put the ice on top of the other ingredients. Put the lid on securely, turn the dial to the smoothie setting (or set the variable speed dial to 1), and start the machine. If using the smoothie setting, process until the machine turns itself off. If using the dial, increase the speed to the highest setting and run for 45 seconds or until completely smooth.

Pour the smoothie into 1 or 2 glasses and serve right away.

½ cup (4 fl oz/125 ml) cold water

½ cucumber, peeled and cut into thirds

½ cup (3 oz/90 g) green grapes

4 oz (125 g) fresh pineapple chunks

1 cup (1 oz/30 g) tightly packed torn, stemmed organic greens

¼ cup (¼ oz/7 g) packed fresh mint leaves

1 cup (8 oz/250 g) ice cubes

OPTIONAL ADD-INS

1 tablespoon honey or agave syrup, or 1 teaspoon granulated Stevia

1 ripe Comice or Bartlett pear, stemmed and cored

1 ripe banana, broken into chunks

½ ripe avocado

1 kiwi, peeled

1-inch (2.5-cm) piece peeled fresh ginger

4 oz (125 g) honeydew cubes

1 tablespoon flax meal, chia seeds, flax oil, coconut oil, or omega-oil blend

Makes about 16 fl oz (500 ml); 1 or 2 servings

clear-skin smoothie

½ cup (4 fl oz/125 ml)
nut milk (page 21), kefir,
or plain Greek yogurt

½ cup (4 fl oz/125 ml) water
(optional)

¼ cup (¾ oz/20 g)
raw rolled oats

1 ripe banana, broken
into chunks

2 teaspoons maple syrup

2 dates, pitted, or ½ ripe pear

1 tablespoon chia seeds or
flax meal (optional)

½ cup (4 oz/125 g) ice cubes

*Makes about 16 fl oz
(500 ml); 1 or 2 servings*

This smoothie may not look beautiful, but the wholesome ingredients in it have been shown to help your skin look luminous. The raw oatmeal adds soluble fiber that may help sweep away impurities in your body along with bad cholesterol. Also, starting your day with a nutritious breakfast is a kickstarter to eating well all day long. Kefir is cultured milk with probiotics. It is low in fat and high in protein and tastes like liquid yogurt. Look for it in health food stores.

Put the nut milk, kefir, or yogurt (plus ½ cup/4 fl oz/125 ml water if using yogurt) into the blender container. Add the oats, banana, maple syrup, dates or pear, and chia seeds or flax meal (if using). Put the ice on top. Put the lid on securely, turn the dial to the smoothie setting (or set the variable speed dial to 1), and start the machine. If using the smoothie setting, process until the machine turns itself off. If using the dial, increase the speed to the highest setting and run for 45 seconds or until completely smooth.

Pour the smoothie into 1 or 2 glasses and serve right away.

carrot-ginger-apple juice

Clean, pure, and simple, this drink is high in antioxidants.
You can double the amount to make two servings, and
you can serve it unstrained if you want it more like
a light smoothie. To strain the juice, a fine sieve works
well; if you don't have one, line a coarse sieve with
a layer of cheesecloth and place over a large liquid
measuring cup to drain.

Cut the apple into quarters; discard the core, seeds, and stem. Cut each
quarter into 2 pieces. Cut the carrot into thirds.

Pour the water into the blender container. Add the apple, carrot,
ginger, and ice. Put the lid on securely, turn the dial to the smoothie
setting (or set the variable speed dial to 1), and start the machine.
If using the smoothie setting, process until the machine turns itself
off. If using the dial, increase the speed to the highest setting and
run for 45 seconds or until completely smooth.

Set a fine-mesh sieve over a measuring cup and pour in the juice; stir
the juice with a rubber spatula until the clear liquid has run through
and only solids remain in the sieve. Pour the juice into a glass and serve.

½ cup (4 fl oz/125 ml)
cold water

1 large Golden Delicious
apple (about 8 oz/250 g)

1 large carrot (about 3 oz/
90 g), peeled

1-inch (2.5-cm) piece fresh
ginger, peeled

½ cup (4 oz/125 g) ice cubes

Makes 1 serving

eggs & roasted asparagus
with lemon-tarragon sabayon

1 bunch asparagus
(about 1 lb/500 g), trimmed

Extra-virgin olive oil

Sea salt or kosher salt

Freshly ground pepper

FOR THE SABAYON

½ shallot, minced

¼ cup (2 fl oz/60 ml)
dry white wine

Kosher salt

1 cup (8 oz/250 g)
unsalted butter,
cut into chunks

2 large eggs

1 egg yolk

3 teaspoons fresh
lemon juice

¼ cup (⅓ oz/10 g) minced
fresh tarragon

12 large eggs

3 tablespoons unsalted
butter, for cooking eggs

6 slices coarse country
bread, toasted

Minced fresh tarragon for
garnish (optional)

Makes 6 servings

One of the miraculous things a Vitamix® machine can do is make sabayon, an-egg rich sauce similar to hollandaise but lighter and fluffier.

Preheat the oven to 450°F (230°C). Line a sheet pan with parchment.

Put the asparagus on the prepared baking sheet. Drizzle with oil and sprinkle with salt and pepper. Toss the asparagus lightly to coat, then spread it out on the sheet and roast until tender, 8–10 minutes.

Meanwhile, make the Sabayon: In a small saucepan, cook the shallot, wine, and a pinch of salt over medium heat until reduced to about 1 tablespoon, about 5 minutes. Add the butter, one chunk at a time, swirling the pan until melted. Pour the contents of the pan into a 1-cup (8 fl oz/250 ml) glass measuring cup with a spout. Crack 2 whole eggs into the blender container then add the egg yolk. Add a pinch of salt and 1 teaspoon of the lemon juice. Put the lid on securely and set the variable speed dial to 4; pulse until the eggs are blended, about 6 times.

Remove the lid plug from the blender lid. With the machine running at variable 4, very slowly pour the butter mixture in a thin stream through the opening (cup your other hand over the hole to prevent spattering). Do not rush this step, or the sauce won't set properly. Continue to pour slowly until every last bit of the butter mixture has been added. Turn off the machine. Put the lid plug back into the lid. Turn the dial to its highest setting and blend until the sauce is steaming hot and whipped, 2 minutes. Scrape the sauce into a bowl, stir in the remaining lemon juice and the tarragon, and cover the bowl to keep warm.

Beat the 12 eggs in a bowl with a little salt and pepper. Melt the 3 tablespoons butter in a nonstick frying pan and cook the eggs over medium heat until softly scrambled. To serve, put a slice of toast on each plate, and top with the scrambled eggs, asparagus, and sabayon. Sprinkle with chopped tarragon, if desired.

chilaquiles & eggs
with roasted chipotle salsa

Invented as a way to use up stale tortillas, chilaquiles are a Mexican comfort food. The sauce gets a deep, smoky flavor from chipotles and charred vegetables.

Place a 10-inch (25-cm) cast-iron or other heavy, uncoated skillet (not nonstick) over medium-high heat. Put the poblano chile, onion, and garlic in the pan and roast, turning as needed with tongs, until charred all over; remove each vegetable from the pan as it is done (the onion and garlic take less time than the chile). Transfer the roasted chile to a bowl, cover with a towel or plastic wrap, and set aside. Peel the garlic.

Put the tomatoes and juice, roasted onion, garlic, chipotle, cumin, oregano, and salt in the blender container. Put the lid on securely, set the dial to variable 1, and start the machine. Slowly increase the speed to 5 and blend until coarsely puréed, about 15 seconds.

Heat the oil in the same pan over medium-high heat. When the oil starts to ripple, carefully pour in the sauce from the blender (it will spatter); set the blender container aside (do not rinse). Cook the purée, stirring, until it thickens, about 5 minutes. Add the tortilla chips, a handful at a time, breaking them up slightly in your hand as you add them, and stir until the mixture is thick but not dry.

Add the water to the blender container, put the lid on securely, set the dial to variable 5, and run the machine for 15 seconds. Pour this mixture into the pan and cook, stirring, until the chilaquiles are almost dry, about 2 minutes. Make 4 depressions in the surface of the chilaquiles with the back of a large spoon and crack an egg into each depression. Cover the pan and cook until the egg whites are set and the yolks are still runny, 3–5 minutes. While the eggs are cooking, peel, stem, and seed the chile, then dice it.

Divide the chilaquiles among 4 shallow bowls, each with an egg. Top with diced chile, crumbled cheese, crema, and cilantro, and serve.

1 fresh poblano chile

½ onion, peeled and root end removed

2 cloves garlic, unpeeled

1 can (14 oz/440 g) diced tomatoes

1 chipotle with adobo sauce (from a can of chipotles in adobo)

½ teaspoon ground cumin

½ teaspoon dried Mexican oregano

½ teaspoon kosher salt

¼ cup (2 fl oz/60 ml) canola oil

About 6 oz (185 g) tortilla chips

1 cup (8 fl oz/250 ml) water

4 large eggs

½ cup (2½ oz/75g) crumbled cotija or feta cheese

½ cup (4 oz/125 g) Mexican crema or sour cream

½ cup (⅔ oz/20 g) chopped fresh cilantro

Makes 4 servings

chocolate-hazelnut butter

8 oz (250 g) hazelnuts (about 1½ cups)

¼ cup (1 oz/30 g) confectioners' sugar

5 oz (155 g) semisweet or bittersweet chocolate, chopped (about 1 cup)

¾ cup (6 fl oz/180 ml) milk (see Note)

2 tablespoons unsalted butter, cut into small pieces

¼ teaspoon sea salt

Makes about 2 cups (20 oz/625 g)

Spread this while it is warm, straight from the blender, on toasted crusty bread for a classic European breakfast or on waffles for a totally American one. This makes enough to use for other purposes, too, such as filling crepes for dessert or eating straight from the jar.

Preheat the oven to 350°F (180°C).

Put the hazelnuts in a pie pan and roast until the skins start to crack and the nuts smell fragrant, 10–12 minutes. Put the nuts in a fine-mesh sieve set in the sink and, with a clean linen or terrycloth tea towel, rub the nuts against the sieve to release the skins (not all the skins will come off). If you don't have a fine-mesh sieve, wrap the nuts in the towel and rub vigorously to release the skins. Put the warm, peeled hazelnuts in the blender container. Add the sugar and chocolate.

Put the milk in a glass measuring cup and microwave on high for 1 minute (or warm it in a small pan on the stove top until it is just hot to the touch). Pour the hot milk into the blender container and add the butter and sea salt. Put the lid on securely and set the variable speed dial to 1. Turn on the machine and gradually increase the speed to the highest setting. Using the tamper to push the ingredients into the blades, blend for 1 minute, then reduce the speed to 7 and blend for 30 seconds more.

If not using right away, scrape the mixture into a jar or other container and let cool to room temperature. Store it, covered, in the refrigerator for up to 1 week.

Note: To make a vegan version, substitute almond or hazelnut milk for the regular milk and coconut oil in place of butter.

eggnog french toast

It's the fresh nutmeg that gives this dish its eggnog-y appeal. If you use cream in the batter, each piece of toast will have a custardy texture, but you can substitute milk for a lower-fat alternative if you prefer. Look for grade B maple syrup for its intense flavor.

Preheat the oven to 200°F (95°C).

Put the eggs, cream, nutmeg, and 1 tablespoon maple syrup in the blender container. Put the lid on securely, set the dial to variable 1, and start the machine. Increase the speed to variable 8 and blend for 30 seconds.

Arrange the bread in a single layer in a large, shallow baking dish or on a rimmed baking sheet. Pour the egg mixture over the bread and let soak for about 5 minutes.

Melt 1 tablespoon butter in each of 1 or 2 frying pans or nonstick skillets or on a griddle. One piece at a time, transfer the soaked bread to the pan(s) and cook until golden-brown on each side, turning once, about 4 minutes total.

Transfer the French toast to a plate and keep warm in the oven. Cook the remaining soaked bread in the same manner, adding butter to the pan as needed. Top each portion with fruit, if desired, and serve with maple syrup.

4 large eggs

½ cup (4 fl oz/125 ml) heavy cream or milk

¼ teaspoon freshly ground nutmeg

Real maple syrup, preferably grade B

8 slices challah or soft white bread

3 tablespoons unsalted butter

Sliced pears or bananas or berries (optional)

Makes 4 servings

puffed oven pancake
with peaches

2 firm-ripe yellow peaches

¼ cup (2 oz/60 g)
unsalted butter

1 tablespoon firmly packed
brown sugar

½ cup (4 fl oz/125 ml)
whole milk

4 large eggs

½ teaspoon almond extract

½ cup (2½ oz/75 g)
all-purpose flour

2 tablespoons
granulated sugar

Confectioners' sugar

Blackberries or raspberries
(optional)

Makes 4–6 servings

The traditional pan used for pancakes is a well-seasoned cast-iron skillet, but an enameled cast-iron frying pan, straight-sided sauté pan or slope-sided all-purpose pan work just fine. Just be sure the pan's handles are ovenproof. When fresh peaches aren't in season, use frozen peaches, fresh firm-but-ripe pears, or even apples instead.

Preheat the oven to 425°F (220°C).

If desired, peel the peaches: Drop the peaches into a pot of boiling water for 30 seconds, then remove with a slotted spoon. Let cool slightly, then pull off the skins. Slice the peeled or unpeeled peaches.

Melt the butter in a 10-inch (25-cm) ovenproof pan over medium-high heat. Add the brown sugar and sliced peaches and cook, stirring occasionally, until the mixture is bubbly and very hot, about 5 minutes.

Meanwhile, put the milk, eggs, almond extract, flour, and granulated sugar in the blender container. Put the lid on securely, turn the variable speed dial to 1, and start the machine. Increase the speed to the highest setting and blend for 30 seconds. Pour the mixture over the sautéed peaches in the hot pan and immediately place the pan in the oven. Bake until the pancake is puffed and golden, 18–20 minutes.

Remove the pan from the oven and sift confectioners' sugar over the pancake. Cut the pancake into wedges and garnish with berries, if desired. Serve right away.

lunch

trio of mediterranean dips
with flatbread

This trio of vegetarian dips makes a great luncheon dish for a casual party, or put them out at a gathering alongside cocktails. The hummus should be blended until smooth; if your blender has a pre-programmed purée feature, it works well for this. The other two dips should be chunkier, so pulse them in short bursts to achieve the right texture. Look for flatbread at well-stocked supermarkets or substitute focaccia, pita bread, or pita crisps.

To prepare the Hummus, put the chickpeas with their liquid in the blender container. Add the garlic, sesame seeds, lemon juice, olive oil, salt, and cayenne. Put the lid on securely, set the dial to the purée setting (or set the variable speed to 1) and start the machine. If using the purée setting, process until the machine stops, using the tamper to push the ingredients into the blades to blend smoothly. If using the dial, increase the speed to the highest setting and process for 1 minute, using the tamper to push the ingredients into the blades to smoothly blend. Taste and adjust the salt and lemon juice. Scrape the purée into a bowl; cover and refrigerate for at least 30 minutes or up to 2 days.

To prepare the Tirosalata, roast the chile directly over a gas burner until it is charred all over, turning with tongs. Place the chile in a bowl, cover with a towel or plastic wrap, and let steam until cool enough to handle. Peel the chile, then cut off the stem, slit the chile open, and remove the seeds and ribs with the back of a knife. Cut the chile into strips.

Put the chile strips in the blender container. Add the yogurt, feta, olive oil, lemon juice, and salt. Put the lid on securely, turn the variable speed dial to 5, and pulse 5 or 6 times, using the tamper to push the ingredients into the blades to coarsely blend. Taste and adjust the salt and lemon juice. Scrape the mixture *continued »*

FOR THE HUMMUS WITH SESAME SEEDS

1 can (15 oz/470 g) chickpeas, undrained

2 cloves garlic

¼ cup (1 oz/30 g) toasted sesame seeds

2 tablespoons freshly squeezed lemon juice

2 tablespoons extra-virgin olive oil

½ teaspoon kosher salt

Pinch of cayenne pepper

FOR THE CREAMY TIROSALATA

1 poblano chile

1 container (6 oz/185 g) plain Greek yogurt

8 oz (250 g) good-quality feta cheese

1 tablespoon extra-virgin olive oil

2 tablespoons freshly squeezed lemon juice

¼ teaspoon kosher salt

1 tablespoon snipped fresh dill

continued >>

trio of dips
continued

FOR THE MUHAMMARA

1½ cups (6 oz/185 g)
walnut halves

1 jar or can (10 or 12 oz/
315 or 375 g) roasted
piquillo peppers, drained

1 clove garlic

1 teaspoon ground cumin

2 tablespoons
fresh lemon juice

Pinch of cayenne pepper

½ teaspoon kosher salt

¼ cup (2 fl oz/60 ml)
extra-virgin olive oil

1 lb (500 g) flatbread

Extra-virgin olive oil

Kosher salt

2 cucumbers, peeled
and sliced (optional)

Makes 8 servings

into a bowl and stir in the dill; cover and refrigerate for at least 30 minutes or up to 2 days.

To prepare the Muhammara, preheat the oven to 350°F (180°C). Put the walnuts in a pie pan and toast in oven until fragrant, 6–8 minutes. Remove them from the oven and let cool slightly.

Put the roasted peppers, garlic, cumin, lemon juice, cayenne, salt, olive oil, and toasted walnuts in the blender container. Put the lid on securely, turn the variable speed dial to 5, and pulse several times, using the tamper to push the ingredients into the blades just until the mixture is smooth but there is some texture left from the nuts. Taste and adjust the salt. Scrape the mixture into a bowl; cover and refrigerate for at least 30 minutes or up to 2 days.

When ready to serve, preheat the oven to 350°F (180°C).

Place the flatbread on 1 or more baking sheets. Brush the flatbread with extra-virgin olive oil and sprinkle lightly with salt. Bake until the bread is warmed through but not crisp, about 12 minutes.

Cut the flatbread into pieces and arrange on a platter with the dips and cucumbers, if using.

white bean pita pockets
with mint, feta & cilantro

This supernutritious, vegetarian filling can be whirled up in seconds. Use it to stuff pita pockets or spread it on toasted country bread. You can also use the bean mixture as a dip for pita crisps or vegetable spears.

Drain the beans and rinse them well with cold water. Cut the green onion into thirds, discarding the root ends but including most of the green tops. Put the beans, green onion, garlic, walnuts, vinegar, oil, cayenne, and a few grinds of pepper in the blender container. Put the lid on securely, turn the variable speed dial to 5, and pulse several times until beans are smooth, but there is some texture left from the nuts. Scrape the mixture into a bowl and stir in the feta (the mixture can be refrigerated, covered, for up to 1 day).

To serve, cut each pita in half crosswise. Tuck one half inside the other (this prevents the pita from splitting when it is filled). Divide the bean mixture among the pita pockets, and then slide 3 cucumber slices into each pocket. Top the bean mixture with the halved cherry tomatoes and a few mint leaves and cilantro sprigs and serve.

1 can (15 oz/470 g) cannellini beans

1 green onion

1 clove garlic

½ cup (2 oz/60 g) chopped walnuts

2 tablespoons red wine vinegar

2 tablespoons olive oil or walnut oil, plus additional for garnish

Pinch of cayenne pepper

Freshly ground black pepper

4 oz (125 g) crumbled feta cheese

4 whole-wheat or regular pita breads

12 slices cucumber

1 cup (6 oz/185 g) small cherry tomatoes, cut in half

Handful of fresh mint leaves

Handful of fresh cilantro sprigs

Makes 4 servings

green goddess soup

1½ cups (12 fl oz/375 ml) buttermilk

1½ lb (24 oz) cucumbers, peeled

1 cup (1 oz/30 g) packed arugula leaves

1 tablespoon packed fresh tarragon leaves, plus additional for garnish (optional)

1 tablespoon white wine vinegar

1 teaspoon sugar

½ teaspoon kosher salt

1 green onion top (green part only)

1 ripe avocado, preferably Hass

½ cup (4 oz/125 g) ice cubes (optional)

Makes 4 servings

In many ways, cool soups are like savory smoothies. Drink this one for a convenient lunch with lots of nutrients. The soup gets its name from its jade-like appearance, achieved by the use of fresh herbs.

Pour the buttermilk into the blender container. Cut the cucumbers into chunks and put them in the container. Add the arugula, tarragon, vinegar, sugar, and salt. Cut the green onion into thirds, discarding the root ends but including most of the green tops, and add them to the container. Cut the avocado in half and remove the pit. With a spoon, scoop the avocado flesh into the container. Put the lid on securely, turn the variable speed dial to 1, and start the machine. Increase the speed to the highest setting and blend until smooth, about 30 seconds. Taste and adjust the salt.

The soup can be served right away, or refrigerated, covered, for up to 6 hours to develop the flavors. If you're serving it immediately and you want a colder soup, add the ice cubes to the mixture when blending. Pour the soup into bowls and garnish with extra tarragon, if desired.

avocado gazpacho
with spicy bread crumbs

Make this smooth, healthful soup even more irresistible by adding texture: Pulse in an avocado at the end and dust each portion with crunchy crumbs. Served in little espresso cups or small glasses, this can also be presented as soup-shot appetizers to make about 12 servings.

To make the Spicy Bread Crumbs, tear the bread into 3 pieces and put them in the blender container. Put the lid on securely and turn the variable speed dial to 5; pulse until fine crumbs form. In a nonstick frying pan, melt the butter over medium-high heat. Add the bread crumbs and sauté until golden, about 1 minute. Add the paprika, salt, and cayenne and continue to sauté until the crumbs are crispy and fragrant, about 1 minute more. Transfer to a plate and let cool.

To make the Gazpacho, put the broth in the blender container. Squeeze the juice from both limes and add it to the container. Add the cilantro and jalapeño. Cut the green onions into thirds, discarding the root ends but including most of the green tops, and add to the container with the cucumber chunks. Cut 1 of the avocadoes in half and remove the pit. With a spoon, scoop the avocado flesh from both halves into the container. Add a pinch of salt and put the ice on top. Put the lid on securely, turn the variable speed dial to 1, and start the machine. Increase the speed to the highest setting and blend until smooth, about 30 seconds. Taste and add salt as needed. If desired, refrigerate the soup, covered, for up to 6 hours to develop the flavors.

To serve, cut the remaining avocado in half and remove the pit. Scoop out the flesh and drop it into the container. Turn the variable speed dial to 3 and pulse about 3 times until the avocado is chopped (the soup will be part smooth and part chunky). Divide the gazpacho among bowls or mugs and sprinkle with the spicy bread crumbs.

FOR THE SPICY BREAD CRUMBS

1 slice soft white sandwich bread

1 tablespoon unsalted butter

¾ teaspoon paprika

½ teaspoon kosher salt

⅛ teaspoon cayenne pepper

FOR THE GAZPACHO

1 cup (8 fl oz/250 ml) low-sodium vegetable or chicken broth

2 limes

½ cup (⅔ oz/20 g) packed fresh cilantro leaves, plus sprigs for garnish

1 small jalapeño pepper, stemmed and seeded

2 green onions

1 English cucumber (about 12 oz/375 g), peeled and cut into chunks

2 ripe avocadoes, preferably Hass

Kosher salt

½ cup (4 oz/125 g) ice cubes (optional)

Makes 4–6 servings

salad in a glass

2 celery stalks

1 green onion

1 small (about 4 oz/125 g) or
½ large red bell pepper

½ cucumber, peeled

1 Roma tomato

1 can (12 oz/375 g) V-8 juice

1 clove garlic

2 tablespoons extra-virgin
olive oil

1 tablespoon fresh
lemon juice

Kosher salt

Hot-pepper sauce

½ cup (4 oz/125 g) ice cubes
(optional)

Makes 2–4 servings

Make this nutritious vegetable drink as coarse or smooth as you like. Served chunky, it will remind you of gazpacho and you may want to use a spoon. Served smooth, it will remind you of liquid salad. It's great with a couple of quesadillas alongside.

Cut the celery stalks crosswise in thirds. Cut the green onion into thirds, discarding the root ends but including most of the green top. Cut the pepper into chunks, discarding the stem and seeds. Cut the cucumber into quarters. Cut the tomato in half.

Pour the V-8 juice into the blender container. Add the celery, green onion, pepper, cucumber, tomato, garlic, olive oil, lemon juice, and a pinch of salt to the container. Put the lid on securely, turn the variable speed dial to 5, and start the machine. Pulse 8–10 times, until the vegetables are finely chopped but not puréed. Remove the lid and check the consistency; if you want it smoother, continue to pulse. Alternatively, for a very smooth texture, purée the mixture by turning the variable speed dial to the highest setting and blending for 30 seconds. Season to taste with hot-pepper sauce and salt.

The soup can be served right away, or refrigerated, covered, for up to 1 day. If you are serving it immediately and you want a colder soup, add the ice cubes to the mixture when blending. Pour into glasses and serve.

asian noodles
with peanut sauce

Often, peanut sauces are thinned with oil, but this version is thinned with warm tea for a lower-fat version. If you use tamari instead of regular soy sauce, the whole dish is gluten-free, too.

In a large pot of boiling salted water, cook the noodles until al dente, about 6 minutes, or according to the package directions. Drain the noodles and rinse under cold water until cool. Shake off the excess water and transfer the noodles to a large bowl. Sprinkle the noodles with the sesame oil and toss to coat. Set aside.

Put 1 cup (8 fl oz/250 ml) of the tea, the peanuts, garlic, ginger, chile, tamari, vinegar, sugar, and red pepper flakes in the blender container. Put the lid on securely, turn the variable speed dial to 1, and start the machine. Slowly increase the speed to variable 8 and blend for 30 seconds; stop the machine and check the consistency—it should be smooth and pourable. If necessary, add the remaining ½ cup (4 fl oz/125 ml) tea and pulse until the right consistency is achieved. Taste and season with salt, if necessary; pulse to blend.

Pour the peanut sauce over the noodles and toss well. Divide the noodles among the bowls, top with the cucumber, green onions, and cilantro leaves, and serve.

Kosher salt

1 lb (500 g) soba (buckwheat) noodles

3 tablespoons sesame oil

1½ cups (12 fl oz/375 ml) warm brewed black tea

1½ cups (9 oz/270 g) dry roasted peanuts

2 cloves garlic

2-inch (5-cm) piece fresh ginger, peeled

1 serrano chile, stemmed and seeded

2 tablespoons tamari or soy sauce

2 tablespoons rice vinegar or red wine vinegar

½ teaspoon sugar

Pinch of red pepper flakes

1 cucumber, peeled, seeded, and diced

2 green onions, thinly sliced

½ cup (⅔ oz/20 g) loosely packed cilantro leaves

Makes 4–6 servings

perfect caesar salad

1 large egg

¼ cup (2 fl oz/60 ml) fresh lemon juice, preferably Meyer lemon

1 anchovy filet

1 clove garlic

2 tablespoons freshly grated Parmigiano-Reggiano cheese, plus additional cheese for shaving or grating

½ cup (4 fl oz/125 ml) extra-virgin olive oil

1 head romaine lettuce, or 2 romaine hearts

1 cup (1½ oz/45g) purchased garlic croutons

Sea salt or kosher salt

Freshly ground pepper

Makes 4–6 servings

To present this restaurant-quality Caesar salad in restaurant style, keep the leaves whole, strew them with croutons, and use a vegetable peeler to shave shards of Parmigiano-Reggiano cheese over each portion. Or, go for a homey look and toss torn leaves, croutons, and grated cheese in a bowl. The dressing gets its creaminess from a soft-boiled egg emulsified by the power of the fast-moving blender blades.

Place the egg in a small saucepan and add water to cover. Bring the water to a gentle boil and cook for 2 minutes. Lift out the egg with a slotted spoon and rinse it under cold water until cool enough to handle.

Meanwhile, put the lemon juice, anchovy, garlic, the 2 tablespoons grated cheese, and the olive oil in the blender container. When the egg is ready, crack it and scoop out the white and yolk directly into the container. Put the lid on securely, turn the variable speed dial to 1, and start the machine. Increase the speed to the highest setting and blend for 45 seconds, until smooth and creamy. Scrape the dressing into a liquid measuring cup (for easy pouring) or other small container and set aside.

Cut the core end off the romaine, wash the leaves, and thoroughly pat them dry. In a large bowl, toss a handful of the whole leaves with some of the dressing (if the dressing has stiffened, whisk it with a fork) then transfer to a plate. Repeat with the remaining leaves and dressing. Arrange the croutons on top, dividing evenly, and shave additional cheese over the top. Season with salt and pepper. Alternatively, after washing the leaves, spin them dry. Tear the leaves into pieces and put them in a salad bowl. Pour the dressing over the lettuce. Toss the leaves very well, then add the croutons and additional grated cheese to taste and toss again. Season with salt and pepper and serve right away.

vietnamese-style vegetable slaw

Turning cabbage into slaw with a Vitamix® machine is much faster than shredding it by hand or in a food processor. The key is to use the wet chop method (see page 13). For more protein than peanuts alone provide, top this salad with cooked chicken or turkey, or tofu.

Set a colander in the sink. Cut each cabbage quarter crosswise in half. Place 2 chunks in the blender container and add enough cold water so that the cabbage floats above the blades. Put the lid on securely and turn the variable speed dial to the highest setting. Pulse once, let the cabbage settle for a moment, then pulse again. Lift out a bit of the cabbage with a slotted spoon to check the consistency; if needed, pulse once more to shred it more finely. Pour the cabbage into the colander to drain. Repeat with the remaining cabbage. Let the cabbage stand in the colander while you prep the remaining vegetables.

Put the pepper chunks in the blender container. Add the green onions and mint. Add enough cold water so that the vegetables float above the blades. Put the lid on securely and turn the variable speed dial to the highest setting. Pulse once, let the ingredients settle for a moment, then pulse again to finely chop. Pour the vegetables into the colander with the cabbage to drain. Lift the colander and shake vigorously to get rid of the excess water, then, with your hands, lift and toss the vegetables in the colander to shake off even more water. Set aside.

Put the lime juice, tamari, fish sauce, oil, sugar, garlic, and chile in the blender container. Put the lid on securely, set the dial to variable speed 1, and start the machine. Increase the speed to 8 and blend for 15 seconds.

Transfer the vegetables from the colander to a large bowl. Pour the dressing over the top and toss very well (at this point, the slaw can be covered and chilled for up to 1 hour; it will get moister as it stands). Divide the slaw among plates and sprinkle each portion with peanuts. Top with the chicken, turkey, or tofu, if using, and serve right away.

1 head regular green or Savoy cabbage, quartered and cored, loose outer leaves removed

1 large red bell pepper, stems, seeds, and ribs removed, cut into chunks

3 green onions, including 1 inch (2.5 cm) of the green tops, cut into thirds

1 cup (1 oz/30 g) loosely packed mint leaves

¼ cup (2 fl oz/60 ml) fresh lime juice

3 tablespoons tamari or soy sauce

2 tablespoons fish sauce

1 tablespoon grapeseed or canola oil

1 tablespoon sugar

1 clove garlic

1 small Thai or bird chile, stem removed

½ cup (2½ oz/75 g) chopped salted peanuts

Cooked chicken or turkey, or tofu (optional)

Makes 4 servings

caprese salad
with tomato-basil vinaigrette

1 ripe Roma tomato

⅓ cup (3 fl oz/80 ml) extra-virgin olive oil

½ cup (½ oz/15 g) lightly packed basil leaves, plus additional for garnish

1 tablespoon white wine vinegar

1 tablespoon balsamic vinegar

Sea salt or kosher salt

1 lb (500 g) mixed heirloom tomatoes, cored and thinly sliced

8 oz (250 g) fresh whole-milk mozzarella or *mozzarella di bufala*, thinly sliced

Freshly ground pepper

Makes 6 servings

Now that there is a rainbow of heirloom tomatoes to choose from, you no longer have to stick to classic red, green, and white for a caprese. Use the ripest and best-tasting heirlooms for the salad, regardless of color.

Cut the Roma tomato in half and put it in the blender container. Add the olive oil, ½ cup (½ oz/15 g) basil leaves, white wine vinegar, balsamic vinegar, and a pinch of salt. Put the lid on securely, turn the variable speed dial to 5, and pulse 5 or 6 times until the vinaigrette is the consistency of a salsa.

Spoon a couple tablespoonfuls of the vinaigrette onto each of 6 plates. Arrange the sliced heirloom tomatoes and mozzarella in an overlapping pattern on top of the dressing. Alternatively, arrange the sliced tomatoes and mozzarella in an overlapping pattern on a serving platter. Spoon the vinaigrette over the tomatoes and cheese.

Season the salad with salt and pepper, garnish with additional basil leaves, and serve right away.

turkey panini
with cranberry relish

Don't wait until Thanksgiving when you can make this satisfying turkey-cranberry sandwich with frozen cranberries any time of the year. Make the relish a day ahead so that the flavors can develop; you'll have enough to use for other meals, too—it's a great accompaniment to chicken, turkey, or pork.

To make the Cranberry Relish, cut the orange, with the peel, into 8 pieces; remove any seeds. Put the orange pieces, cranberries, and ginger into the blender container. Add enough cold water so that the fruit floats above the blades. Put the lid on securely and turn the variable speed dial to the highest setting. Pulse 5 or 6 times, until the fruit is finely chopped. Pour the chopped fruit into a fine-mesh sieve or colander to drain. Shake the sieve vigorously to get rid of excess water. Put the drained fruit in a bowl and stir in the sugar. Cover the relish and refrigerate for at least 1 day or up to 5 days.

Preheat a panini press, ridged stove-top grill pan, or griddle. Arrange the bread slices on a sheet of parchment paper. Butter 1 side of each slice, then turn the slices over and swipe the unbuttered sides with mayonnaise and horseradish to taste. Sprinkle about 2 tablespoons of the cheese on each slice (this helps to "glue" the sandwich together). Top four of the slices with turkey, and then put a heaping tablespoon of cranberry relish in the center of each turkey slice (it will spread out when pressed). Invert the remaining slices of bread over the turkey and relish so that the buttered side is facing up. One at a time, transfer the sandwiches to the panini press or pan. If using a panini press, close it and cook until the bread is golden-brown and crisp and cheese is melted, 3–5 minutes. If using a ridged grill pan or griddle, place a pot lid directly on the sandwiches to weigh them down and cook, turning once, until golden-brown and cheese is melted, 4–6 minutes total.

Cut each sandwich in half. Pass additional cranberry relish at the table.

FOR THE CRANBERRY RELISH

1 organic navel or juice orange (about 8 oz/250 g)

2 cups (8 oz) frozen cranberries

1-inch (2.5-cm) piece fresh ginger, peeled

⅔ cup (5 oz/155 g) sugar

FOR THE PANINI

8 slices good-quality white bread

2 tablespoons butter, at room temperature

Mayonnaise

Prepared horseradish

1 cup (4 oz/125 g) grated Monterey jack, white cheddar, or Asiago cheese

¾ lb (375 g) thinly sliced roast turkey, ham, or pork tenderloin

Makes 4 servings

dinner

provençal fennel
& red pepper soup

Hot soups are quick to make in a Vitamix® Professional Series™ blender. This version offers lots of nutrients from colorful, fresh vegetables and seasonings inspired by those you find in the south of France.

Trim the tops from the fennel, reserving a few fronds for garnish. Cut the fennel bulb into quarters and remove the core; slice the fennel thinly. Melt the butter in a sauté pan over medium-high heat; add the fennel, onion, and a pinch of salt, and sauté until sizzling, 1–2 minutes. Reduce the heat to low and cover the pan; cook until the vegetables are soft but not brown, 8–10 minutes.

Meanwhile, if using fresh tomatoes, peel, seed, and chop them. Drain the red peppers and rinse under running cold water; pat dry.

Pour the broth into the blender container. Scrape the fennel and onion from the pan into the container. Add the tomatoes with their juices, roasted peppers, fennel seeds, and cream. Put the lid on securely and turn the dial to the Hot Soup program. Blend until the machine turns itself off (this takes about 5 minutes; steam will rise from the lid when it is finished). Taste and add salt as needed to balance the flavors; pulse once or twice to blend.

Serve the soup right away or, if you prefer it hotter, transfer the soup to a saucepan and heat through on the stove top. Divide the soup among bowls and garnish with the fennel fronds.

1 lb (500 g) fresh fennel
(1 large or 2 small bulbs)

2 tablespoons unsalted
butter

½ yellow onion, chopped

Kosher salt

1 lb (500 g) ripe red tomatoes
or 1 can (14 oz/430 g) plum
tomatoes

1 jar (12 oz/375 g) roasted
red peppers

2 cups (16 fl oz/500 ml)
low-sodium vegetable
or chicken broth

¼ teaspoon fennel seeds

½ cup (4 fl oz/125 ml)
heavy cream

Makes 4 servings

thai-style curried squash soup

½ butternut squash (about 12 oz/375 g), or ¾ lb (375 g) peeled, cubed fresh or frozen butternut squash

1 navel orange

1 lime

1 can (about 14 oz/440 g) unsweetened coconut milk (not light)

1 lemongrass stalk

2 cloves garlic

1 shallot, cut into chunks

2-inch (5-cm) piece fresh ginger, peeled

1 serrano chile, stemmed and seeded

1 tablespoon curry powder

1 cup (8 fl oz/250 ml) low-sodium chicken broth

Kosher salt

1–2 teaspoons golden brown sugar

Créme fraîche or fresh cilantro leaves for garnish (optional)

Makes 6–8 servings

Roasting the squash first enhances its flavor. If you're tight on time, use peeled butternut squash, either frozen or vacuum-packed. You can also serve this as an appetizer for 10–12 people in little espresso cups.

To roast the squash, preheat the oven to 375°F (190°C). Place the squash half (flesh-side down) or the squash cubes on a parchment-lined baking sheet. Roast until the squash is soft and browned in spots, about 45 minutes for the halved squash or about 25 minutes for the cubes. Remove from the oven. If using the squash half, let it cool slightly, then turn it over and scoop out the seeds with a spoon. Rake the flesh from the skin with a fork and transfer it to a bowl.

Finely grate 1 teaspoon zest from the orange and add it to the blender container. Squeeze the juice from both the orange and the lime into the container. Add the coconut milk. Cut the bottom ½ inch (12 mm) off the lemongrass stalk and discard it. Cut a 3-inch (7.5-cm) piece of the stalk just above this and peel off the outer layer. With the side of a heavy knife, crush the lemongrass to release its flavor. Put the lemongrass, garlic, shallot, ginger, chile, and curry powder in the blender container. Turn the dial to the smoothie setting (or set the variable speed dial to 1), and start the machine. If using the smoothie setting, process until the machine turns itself off. If using the dial, increase the speed to the highest setting and process for 45 seconds.

Add the broth and squash to the blender container. Put the lid on securely and turn the dial to the Hot Soup program. Blend until the machine turns itself off (this takes about 5 minutes; steam will rise from lid when it is finished). Taste and add salt and brown sugar as needed to balance the flavors; pulse once or twice to blend.

Serve right away, or, if you prefer it hotter, transfer the soup to a saucepan and heat through on the stove top. Divide the soup among bowls and garnish with a swirl of crème fraîche or cilantro.

warm potato-leek soup
with bacon crumbles

There's no need for cream in this soup; the action of the blender purées the potato so smoothly, that it's just as rich without the cream. If you don't have a microwave to cook the potato, bake it in a 350°F (180°C) oven until tender, 45 minutes to 1 hour.

Cook the bacon in a nonstick frying pan over medium-high heat until crisp. While the bacon is cooking, cut the leek in half lengthwise and rinse thoroughly under cold water to remove any grit. Slice the leek crosswise and set aside.

Drain the bacon on paper towels and discard the fat from the pan. Add the butter to the pan and melt it over medium heat. When the butter has melted, add the leeks and cook, stirring occasionally, until soft and golden, about 7 minutes.

While the leeks are cooking, using a fork, poke a few holes in the potato. Microwave the potato on high for 7 minutes, or until tender.

Pour the broth into the blender container. When the leeks are ready, scrape them into the blender container. Cut the cooked potato in half and remove the peel (use a paring knife, as the potato will be hot); cut the potato flesh into chunks. Add the potato and cubed cheese to the container. Put the lid on securely and turn the dial to the Hot Soup program. Blend until the machine turns itself off (this takes about 5 minutes; steam will rise from the lid when it is finished). While the soup blends, crumble or mince the bacon strips.

Pour the soup into bowls or mugs, sprinkle each with bacon and chives, and serve right away.

3 slices thick-cut bacon

1 leek, white part only

2 tablespoons unsalted butter

1 large russet potato

4 cups (32 fl oz/1 l) low-sodium vegetable or chicken broth

4 oz (125 g) white Cheddar cheese, cubed

Finely snipped fresh chives for garnish

Makes 4–6 servings

pappa al pomodoro
(tuscan-style tomato soup)

3 tablespoons extra-virgin
olive oil, plus more for
drizzling

1 small red or
yellow onion, sliced

3 cloves garlic, sliced

9 fresh basil leaves

Kosher salt

Pinch of red pepper flakes

4 cups (32 fl oz/1 l) water

1 lb (500 g) ripe red
tomatoes, peeled and
seeded, or 1 can
(14 oz/430 g) peeled
San Marzano tomatoes

2 tablespoons tomato paste

4 oz (125 g) day-old
Italian bread

Freshly grated
Parmesan cheese

Makes 4 servings

Hailing from Tuscany, which is known for its bread-thickened dishes, this soup can be eaten warm or at room temperature in the summer when tomatoes are at their peak. Traditionally it's served nearly dense enough to eat with a fork, but this version is looser. Dust each bowl with cheese and dig in with a spoon.

Warm the 3 tablespoons olive oil in a small frying pan over medium heat. Add the onion, garlic, 5 of the basil leaves, ½ teaspoon salt, and the red pepper flakes and sauté until the onion and garlic are very soft but not browned, about 10 minutes, turning down the heat if the onion or garlic starts to brown. Remove from the heat.

Add the water to the blender container. Scrape the contents of the pan into the container. Add the tomatoes and tomato paste. Put the lid on securely and turn the dial to the Hot Soup program. Blend until the machine turns itself off (this takes about 5 minutes; steam will rise from the lid when it is finished). While the machine is running, cut or tear the bread into 1-inch (2.5-cm) pieces.

When the machine has stopped, remove the lid and add the bread pieces. Put the lid back on securely, turn the dial to variable speed 4, and pulse 3 or 4 times to chop the bread, without puréeing. Taste and add more salt if needed.

Divide the soup among soup bowls, drizzle each with olive oil, and sprinkle with Parmesan. Garnish each bowl with 1 of the remaining basil leaves and serve.

meatballs
in tomato-cream sauce

These plump meatballs are a great main course on their own, but become a whole meal when served over pasta such as penne or farfalle, or rice. When finished, the sauce may look more rosy than red, which is caused by the aeration from the blender's powerful motor.

Put the bread crumbs in a large bowl and add the milk. Set aside until the bread softens, about 5 minutes. Add the ground beef, ground pork, parsley, garlic, Worcestershire sauce, and salt to the bowl. With your hands, knead the mixture very well (at first it will seem wet; keep working it until it is no longer damp). Shape the mixture into 12 even-size balls and set aside.

Warm 3 tablespoons of the oil in a wide sauté pan or frying pan over medium-high heat. Add the onion and sauté until softened and just golden, about 5 minutes. Pour in the wine and cook until the liquid is nearly evaporated, 1–2 minutes. Scrape the mixture into the blender container. Add the tomatoes with their juices, tomato paste, and cream. Put the lid on securely and turn the dial to the Hot Soup program. Blend until the machine turns itself off (this takes about 5 minutes; steam will rise from the lid when it is finished).

Meanwhile, wipe out the pan, pour in the remaining 2 tablespoons oil, and warm over high heat. When the oil is shimmering, add the meatballs and sear, without turning, until they are browned on the bottom and release easily from pan when turned with tongs (at this point, the sauce in the blender will be done). Turn the meatballs over and, if desired, pour off the fat in the pan. Pour the sauce from the blender into the pan. Reduce the heat, cover, and simmer the meatballs in the sauce until cooked through, about 15 minutes.

To serve, ladle the meatballs and sauce into bowls and garnish with torn basil leaves and Parmesan cheese.

1 cup (1½ oz/45 g) panko breadcrumbs

½ cup (4 fl oz/125 ml) milk

¾ pound (375 g) ground beef

¾ pound (375 g) ground pork

¼ cup (¼ oz/7 g) finely chopped fresh flat-leaf parsley

2 cloves garlic, pressed

2 tablespoons Worcestershire sauce

1 teaspoon kosher salt

5 tablespoons (3 fl oz/80 ml) olive oil

1 yellow onion, chopped

½ cup (4 fl oz/125 ml) dry white wine

1 can (28 oz/875 g) peeled San Marzano tomatoes

1 tablespoon tomato paste

¼ cup (4 fl oz/125 ml) heavy cream

Torn fresh basil leaves and freshly grated Parmesan cheese for serving

Makes 4–6 servings

turkish-style grilled chicken
with tomato-mint salad

¼ cup (2 fl oz/60 ml) water

1 cup (8 oz/250 g) plain
Greek yogurt

2 tablespoons fresh
lemon juice

1 tablespoon extra-virgin
olive oil

2 cloves garlic

½ shallot, cut into chunks

1 tablespoon chili powder

¾ teaspoon ground cumin

½ teaspoon cayenne

1 teaspoon kosher salt

½ teaspoon black pepper

6 skinless, boneless chicken
breast halves, cubed

TOMATO-MINT SALAD
1 basket (about 8 oz/250 g)
Sweet 100 cherry tomatoes

2 cups (2 oz/60 g) fresh
mint leaves

3 tablespoons extra-virgin
olive oil

1 tablespoon freshly
squeezed lemon juice

1 clove garlic, pressed

Kosher salt

Makes 6 servings

Yogurt-based marinades are traditional for chicken throughout the eastern Mediterranean. If you don't want to skewer the chicken, you can simply grill the half breasts or roast them on a rack set over a foil-lined baking sheet in a 450°F (230°C) oven for 20–25 minutes. Thinly slice the chicken breasts crosswise and top with the salad.

Put the water, yogurt, lemon juice, olive oil, garlic, shallot, chili powder, cumin, cayenne, salt, and pepper in the blender container. Put the lid on securely, turn the variable speed dial to 1, and start the machine. Increase the speed to the highest setting and blend for 30 seconds. Place the chicken in a glass or plastic container and pour the marinade over the chicken. Turn the chicken until coated. Cover and let stand at room temperature for 30 minutes or refrigerate, covered, for up to 3 hours. Soak bamboo skewers in water to cover.

Stem the tomatoes and cut them in half lengthwise. Roughly chop the mint. In a bowl, toss together the tomatoes, mint, olive oil, lemon juice, garlic, and salt to taste.

Prepare a grill for direct-heat cooking over medium-high heat. Meanwhile, drain the skewers. Lift the chicken pieces from the marinade and thread onto the skewers. Oil the grill rack. Grill the chicken skewers, turning once, until the meat is no longer pink in the center, 12–15 minutes.

Arrange the chicken skewers and the Tomato-Mint Salad on a platter and serve right away.

roasted salmon
with kale pesto & farro

This all-in-one dinner is surprisingly efficient to put together when you use your blender for both the farro and the pesto. Putting a little warm water in the pesto makes it creamy.

Put the onion, celery, and carrot chunks in the blender container. Add enough cold water so that vegetables float above the blades. Put the lid on securely and turn the variable speed dial to the highest setting. Pulse once, let the ingredients settle for a moment, then pulse again to finely chop. Drain the vegetables in a colander and shake well.

In a wide sauté pan, warm 3 tablespoons oil over medium-high heat. Add the chopped vegetables and sauté until tender, about 3 minutes. Add the farro and stir for 1 minute to coat with oil. Add the broth, 1½ cups (12 fl oz/375 ml) water, and a pinch of salt and bring to a boil. Reduce the heat to low, cover, and simmer until the broth is absorbed and the grains are chewy, 35–40 minutes, stirring occasionally. (If necessary, uncover and cook, stirring, to evaporate the last bit of liquid.)

Meanwhile, preheat the oven to 450°F (230°C). Sprinkle the salmon with salt. Set a rimmed baking sheet lined with foil in the oven to heat.

To make the Kale Pesto, put the warm water, oil, kale, Parmesan, pine nuts, garlic, orange zest, and a pinch of salt in the blender container. Put the lid on securely, turn the dial to variable speed 1, and start the machine. Increase the speed to the highest setting and blend for about 20 seconds, using the tamper to push the ingredients into the blades until smooth. Transfer to a bowl.

Remove the heated baking sheet from the oven and lightly brush the foil with olive oil. Place the salmon, skin side down, on the foil. Roast until the salmon is just pink inside, 8–10 minutes. Divide the farro among plates, spooning it on one side of each plate. Spoon some pesto on the other side of each plate and place a salmon filet on top. Pass the remaining pesto at the table.

½ yellow onion, cut into chunks

1 celery stalk, cut into chunks

1 carrot, cut into chunks

3 tablespoons olive oil, plus more for cooking the salmon

1 cup (6 oz/185 g) farro

1 cup (8 fl oz/250 ml) low-sodium chicken broth

1½ cups (12 fl oz/375 ml) water

Kosher salt

4 skin-on salmon filets, about 6 oz (185 g) each

FOR THE KALE PESTO
¼ cup (2 fl oz/60 ml) warm water

⅓ cup (3 fl oz/80 ml) extra-virgin olive oil

1½ cups (1½ oz/45 g) lightly packed torn Tuscan kale leaves, stems discarded

⅓ cup (1¼ oz/40 g) freshly grated Parmesan cheese

¼ cup (1¼ oz/40 g) pine nuts, toasted

1 clove garlic

1 teaspoon grated orange zest

Kosher salt

Makes 4 servings

cuban-style pork

½ cup (4 fl oz/125 ml) warm water

1 seedless navel orange

1 clove garlic

2 teaspoons paprika

1 teaspoon ground cumin

1 teaspoon kosher salt

½ teaspoon dried thyme

¼ cup (2 fl oz/60 ml) olive oil

2 pork tenderloins, about 1½ lb (750 g) total

2 tablespoons unsalted butter

Makes 4–6 servings

This vibrant blend of whole citrus segments doubles as both a marinade and a sauce for grilled pork tenderloin. Serve the sliced pork with cooked rice and black beans.

Pour the warm water into the blender container. With a vegetable peeler, remove a 4-inch (10-cm) piece of the orange peel and put it in the blender container. With a sharp knife, cut off the ends of the orange and trim away the remaining peel and white pith; cut the fruit into quarters. Add the fruit to the container along with the garlic, paprika, cumin, salt, thyme, and olive oil. Put the lid on securely, turn the variable speed dial to 1, and start the machine. Increase the speed to the highest setting and blend for 30 seconds until puréed.

Put the tenderloins in a container that fits them snugly. Pour in just enough of the mixture from the blender to coat (about ⅓ cup/3 fl oz/ 80 ml). Turn the meat in the marinade to coat well. Cover and let stand at room temperature for up to 1 hour, or refrigerate for up to 3 hours. Transfer the extra marinade to a covered container and refrigerate.

Prepare a grill for direct-heat cooking over high heat or preheat the oven to 450°F (230°C). Oil the grill rack, or line a rimmed baking sheet with foil and place a metal rack on the sheet.

Lift the pork from the marinade and grill, turning once, until the meat is cooked through, about 20 minutes. Alternatively, roast the pork until cooked to your liking, 18–20 minutes for medium-rare. Let the meat stand for 5 minutes before slicing.

Warm the reserved marinade in a small saucepan over medium-high heat. Whisk in the butter until melted; season with salt. Slice the meat and spoon the sauce over each portion.

grilled lamb chops
with chimichurri

Lightning fast and impressive, chimichurri sauce is a staple in Argentina, where it is served with grilled steaks. The herbal flavors are fantastic with grilled lamb, too. You can use meaty chops from the leg or shoulder; rib chops from the rack are a bit delicate for chimichurri. When measuring the parsley and cilantro, cut the leaves off at an angle and don't worry if some stems get in there; they are full of flavor.

Prepare a grill for direct-heat cooking over medium-high heat or preheat the broiler. If using the broiler, line a broiler pan with foil. Put the lamb chops on a plate, sprinkle both sides with salt, and let the meat stand while you make the chimichurri.

Put the olive oil, grapeseed oil, and vinegar in the blender container. Add the garlic, red pepper flakes, parsley, cilantro, oregano, and ½ teaspoon salt. Put the lid on securely. Turn the dial to variable speed 3 and pulse 10 times, using the tamper to push the ingredients into the blades as you work, until the herbs are finely chopped but not puréed. Pour the sauce into a bowl.

Grill or broil the lamb chops, turning once, until cooked to your liking, about 7 minutes for medium-rare. Let the chops stand for a few minutes before serving.

Arrange the lamb chops on a warmed platter. Spoon a few tablespoons of the chimichurri over each chop. Pass the remaining chimichurri at the table.

6 lamb chops

Kosher salt

½ cup (4 fl oz/125 ml) extra-virgin olive oil

⅓ cup (3 fl oz/80 ml) grapeseed or canola oil

⅓ cup (3 fl oz/80 ml) sherry wine vinegar or red wine vinegar

2 cloves garlic

½ teaspoon red pepper flakes

1 cup (1 oz/30 g) tightly packed fresh parsley

1 cup (1 oz/30 g) tightly packed fresh cilantro

¼ cup (⅓ oz/10 g) loosely packed fresh oregano leaves

Makes 6 servings

ricotta tortellini
with spinach-gorgonzola sauce

Kosher salt

2 tablespoons
unsalted butter

2 tablespoons
minced shallot

4 oz (125 g)
baby spinach leaves

1 cup (8 fl oz/250 ml)
heavy cream

4 oz (125 g) Gorgonzola
dolce cheese

20 oz (625 g) regular
(not spinach) tortellini
with ricotta filling

Shaved or grated
Parmesan cheese

Freshly ground pepper
(optional)

Makes 4–6 servings

In Bologna, home of the richest pasta dishes in Italy, spinach tortellini are often topped with Gorgonzola cream sauce. This recipe inverts that scenario: White tortellini sport emerald-green sauce instead of the other way around. If you can find it, use Gorgonzola dolce cheese, which is softer and sweeter than regular Gorgonzola or other sharp blue cheeses.

Bring a large pot of salted water to a vigorous boil. Meanwhile, in a 7- to 10-inch (18- to 25-cm) frying pan, melt the butter over medium-high heat. Add the shallots and sauté until softened, about 30 seconds. Add the spinach, a handful at a time, stirring until each batch wilts. When all the spinach has been wilted, remove the pan from the heat.

Pour the cream into the blender container, then scrape in the spinach. Put the lid on securely and turn the dial to the Hot Soup program. Blend until the machine turns itself off (this takes about 5 minutes; steam will rise from the lid when it is finished). Remove the lid and add the Gorgonzola; put the lid back on. Turn the variable speed to 4 and pulse about 6 times to blend in the cheese.

Cook the tortellini in the boiling water for 2 minutes less than the time indicated on the package, or until just before it becomes al dente. Drain the tortellini and return it to the pot; pour in the sauce from the blender. Place the pot over medium-high heat and cook, stirring, until the sauce is thickened and the tortellini are al dente, about 2 minutes.

Divide the sauced pasta among warmed wide, shallow bowls, top with Parmesan and pepper, if using, and serve right away.

dessert

caffe latte cocktail shake

This is a grown-up dessert, perfect for easy entertaining. For a stronger cocktail, substitute all liqueur rather than the coffee-Kahlua blend.

Preheat the oven to 350°F (180°C). Spread the coconut in a pie pan and toast in the oven until golden-brown, stirring once or twice, 8–10 minutes. Alternatively, stir the coconut in a small, nonstick skillet over medium heat until golden-brown, about 5 minutes. Let the coconut cool. (Toasted coconut keeps, covered, for several days at room temperature.)

Put the milk, coffee, and liqueur in the blender container. Add the ice cream. Put the lid on securely, turn the variable speed dial to 1, and start the machine. Increase the speed to variable 8 and blend for 15 seconds, until smooth and frothy.

Divide the ice cream mixture among cocktail glasses and top with whipped cream and the toasted coconut. Offer a spoon to stir the elements together.

¼ cup (2 oz/60 g) flaked coconut

⅓ cup (3 fl oz/80 ml) whole milk

2 tablespoons strong brewed coffee or espresso, cooled

¼ cup (2 fl oz/60 ml) coffee-flavored liqueur, such as Kahlua

1½ pints (21 oz/660 g) vanilla or coffee ice cream

Whipped cream

Makes 6 servings

silken chocolate mousse

1 lb (16 oz/500 g) silken tofu

6 oz (185 g) top-quality bittersweet chocolate, chopped

¼ cup (2 fl oz/60 ml) chilled unsweetened coconut milk (not light)

3 tablespoons real maple syrup (preferably grade B)

1 teaspoon vanilla extract

¼ teaspoon almond extract

Pinch of sea salt

Sliced almonds, fresh berries, or chocolate shavings for garnish (optional)

Makes 4 servings

No one will know this dessert is vegan, and no one will care because it is ultrarich and luscious. The secret ingredient is silken tofu, which replaces the typical eggs and cream used to make mousse. Put the can of coconut milk in the refrigerator instead of the cupboard when you buy it so that you can have chilled coconut milk on hand; use the leftover milk for the Fresh Berries with Warm White-Chocolate Cream (page 91).

Place four ¾ cup (6 fl oz/180 ml) bowls, ramekins, or glass jars on a baking sheet or tray. Remove the tofu from the package, discarding the liquid; place the tofu on a paper towel–lined plate to drain.

Melt the chocolate in a metal bowl set over a pan of barely simmering water; do not let the bottom of the bowl touch the water. Pour the coconut milk into the blender container, then scrape in the melted chocolate. Add the drained tofu, maple syrup, vanilla extract, almond extract, and a pinch of sea salt. Put the lid on securely, turn the variable speed dial to 1, and start the machine. Increase the speed to variable 5 and blend for 15 seconds. Remove the lid and scrape down the sides of the container, then cover and increase the speed to variable 8 and blend again for 30 seconds to aerate the mixture.

Divide the mousse among the bowls, filling each about three-fourths full. Cover the bowls and refrigerate until the mousse is set, at least 2 hours and up to 1 day.

When ready to serve, garnish with almonds, fresh berries, or chocolate shavings, if desired.

butterscotch chiffon pudding
with toffee crunch

This is a worry-free egg custard: Using the Hot Soup program, the eggs are cooked to a safe temperature without curdling. For a nice contrast, top with chopped toffee candy.

In a very small bowl, whisk the gelatin with the cold water to soften. Place six ¾-cup (6–fl oz/180-ml) ramekins or glass jars on a baking sheet or tray. Set aside.

In a saucepan, melt the butter over medium heat. Cook until the foam subsides and the butter starts to turn a light nut-brown, 3–5 minutes. Whisk in the brown sugar and vanilla, then pour in the milk. Stir over medium heat for 1 minute or until the milk is warm. Pour the mixture into the blender container; add the egg yolks and sea salt. Put the lid on securely and turn the dial to the Hot Soup program. Blend until the machine turns itself off (this takes about 5 minutes; steam will rise from the lid when it is finished). Remove the lid, scrape the gelatin mixture into the container, put the lid back on securely, and turn the dial to variable speed 4. Pulse 5 or 6 times to blend in the gelatin. Pour the mixture into a bowl (if any gelatin lumps remain, whisk until blended).

Clean and dry the blender container and pour in the cream. Put the lid on securely, turn the dial to variable speed 1, and start the machine. Increase the speed to the highest setting and blend for 10 seconds, until the cream is lightly whipped. Fold the whipped cream into the custard-gelatin mixture until completely blended. Pour the mixture through a fine-mesh sieve into a 4-cup (32–fl oz/1-l) glass measuring cup (or back into the container) to get rid of the foam and make it easy to pour. Pour the mixture into the ramekins, filling each about three-fourths full. Cover the ramekins with plastic wrap, then transfer to the refrigerator and chill until set, at least 4 hours or up to 1 day.

To serve, sprinkle a tablespoon of the crushed toffee on top of each pudding; if desired, top with whipped cream.

1 envelope gelatin

3 tablespoons cold water

¼ cup (2 oz/60 g) unsalted butter

¾ cup (6 oz/185 g) firmly packed dark brown sugar

1 tablespoon vanilla extract

1 cup (8 fl oz/250 ml) milk

4 egg yolks

Pinch sea salt

1 cup (8 fl oz/250 ml) chilled heavy cream

6 tablespoons (about 1¾ oz/ 55 g) English toffee bits

Whipped cream for garnish (optional)

Makes 6 servings

pumpkin bread puddings
with maple crème anglaise

FOR THE CRÈME ANGLAISE
½ cup *each* (4 fl oz/125 ml)
whole milk and heavy cream

½ vanilla bean

3 large egg yolks

¼ cup (2 oz/60 g) sugar

2 tablespoons real maple
syrup, preferably grade B

FOR THE BREAD PUDDINGS
Butter for greasing

6 slices white sandwich bread,
crusts removed, quartered

1 cup (8 fl oz/250 ml)
heavy cream

½ cup (4 fl oz/125 ml)
whole milk

½ cup (3½ oz/105 g)
firmly packed brown sugar

2 tablespoons
granulated sugar

¾ cup (5½ oz/170 g) canned
unsweetened pumpkin purée

3 large eggs,
at room temperature

1 tablespoon vanilla extract

¾ teaspoon ground cinnamon

½ teaspoon *each*
ground cloves and freshly
grated nutmeg

Kosher salt

Makes 6 servings

Somewhere between a warm pudding and a soufflé, this is a great alternative to the holiday pumpkin pie. Double the recipe to feed a crowd.

To prepare the Crème Anglaise, put the milk and cream in a glass measuring cup and microwave on high for 1 minute (or warm on the stove top until it is warm to the touch). With a paring knife, slit the vanilla bean lengthwise and scrape the seeds from the inside into the milk mixture. Put the milk mixture, egg yolks, and sugar in the blender container. Put the lid on securely and turn the dial to the Hot Soup program. Blend until the machine turns itself off (this takes about 5 minutes; steam will rise from the lid when it is finished). Add the maple syrup and pulse once or twice on variable speed 1; transfer the mixture to a pitcher or other container. (At this point, the Crème Anglaise can be cooled, covered, and refrigerated for up to 2 days.) If making the puddings right away, wash the blender container.

Preheat the oven to 350°F (180°C). Generously butter six ¾-cup (6 fl–oz/ 180-ml) ramekins or custard cups and set them on a baking sheet.

Put the cream, milk, brown sugar, granulated sugar, pumpkin, eggs, vanilla, cinnamon, clove, nutmeg, and a pinch of salt in the blender container. Put the lid on securely, set the dial to variable 1, and start the machine. Increase the speed to variable 5 and blend for 15 seconds. Add the bread pieces to the container; put the lid back on securely, turn the dial to variable 8, and blend for 20 seconds. Divide the mixture among the prepared ramekins, filling each ramekin almost to the top. (At this point, the bread puddings can be covered with plastic wrap and refrigerated for up to 1 day. Bring them to room temperature before baking.) Bake the puddings until puffed and just set in the center, about 35 minutes.

To serve, pour some Crème Anglaise over the top of each warm pudding. Pass the remaining Crème Anglaise at the table.

mango-ginger sherbet

1 cup (8 fl oz/250 ml) buttermilk

½ cup (4 oz/125 g) sugar

1 or 3 pieces Australian crystallized ginger (see Note)

1 small banana, peeled and broken into pieces, frozen

2 ripe mangoes, about 1 lb (500 g) total, peeled, diced, and frozen, or 14 oz (440 g) frozen mango pieces

Makes 6 servings

Creamy, tangy, and a little tropical, try this after a spicy meal. Since you need to freeze the banana, take the opportunity to cut up a mango and freeze it, too, for outstanding flavor (or use frozen mangoes or peaches).

Put the buttermilk, sugar, ginger, banana, and mango in the blender container. Put the lid on securely and turn the dial to the Frozen Dessert program. Turn the machine on and blend, using the tamper to push the ingredients into the blades, until the machine turns itself off.

Serve right away (the sherbet will be soft) or transfer to a freezer container, cover, and freeze until firm, up to 4 days.

Note: Australian crystallized ginger is sold either in thick slices, in which case you need one, or in cubes, in which case you need three.

mexican chocolate sorbet

Though it tastes rich, this spicy sorbet is very low in fat. By using the Hot Soup program on the Vitamix® Professional Series™ blender, the chocolate is melted and the mixture is aerated, so you don't need to use a separate ice cream maker.

In a saucepan, bring the water to a boil. Add the sugar and stir until dissolved. Remove from the heat.

Pour the sugar mixture into the blender container. Add the chocolate, cocoa powder, vanilla, cinnamon, chile powder, and salt. Put the lid on securely and turn the dial to the Hot Soup program. Blend until the machine turns itself off (this takes about 5 minutes; steam will rise from the lid when it is finished). Pour the mixture into a shallow, freezer-safe container. Let stand, uncovered, at room temperature until cool, then cover and transfer to the freezer until very firm, at least 6 hours or up to 5 days.

To serve, let the sorbet soften slightly at room temperature, then scoop into serving portions.

2 cups (16 fl oz/500 ml) water

1 cup (0 oz/250 g) sugar

3 oz (90 g) top-quality bittersweet chocolate, coarsely chopped

½ cup (1½ oz/45 g) unsweetened natural cocoa powder

2 teaspoons vanilla extract

¼ teaspoon ground cinnamon

⅛ teaspoon ancho chile powder or a pinch of cayenne pepper

Pinch of sea salt

Makes 6 servings

cherry-almond sorbetto

What distinguishes Italian sorbets served in the best gelaterias is the intensity of the fruit factor: You order cherry sorbetto and what you taste is cherries. The addition of a little almond extract just amplifies that.

Combine the orange juice, cherries, sugar, and almond extract in the blender container. Put the lid on securely, turn the dial to variable speed 1, and start the machine. Increase the speed to variable 5 and blend for 30 seconds, using the tamper to push the ingredients into the blades, until the mixture is smooth, but there is still some texture from the fruit. Transfer the mixture to a freezer container, cover, and freeze for at least 4 hours or up to 4 days.

½ cup (4 fl oz/125 g) fresh orange juice (from 1 large navel orange)

1 lb (500 g) frozen pitted dark cherries, such as Bing

⅓ cup (3 oz/90 g) sugar

½ teaspoon almond extract

Makes 8 servings

peach-raspberry ice cream

½ cup (4 fl oz/125 ml) whole milk

½ cup (4 fl oz/125 ml) heavy cream

3 egg yolks

⅓ cup (3 oz/90 g) sugar

1 teaspoon vanilla extract

1 cup (4 oz/125 g) frozen peach slices

1 cup (4 oz/125 g) frozen raspberries

Makes 6 servings

This is the real deal: rich, custardy, homemade ice cream, made without an ice cream maker. Make the base the day before and chill it, then you can whip up the ice cream instantly. You can make it all peach, or all raspberry, but the combination of the two is hard to beat.

Put the milk and cream in a glass measuring cup and microwave on high for 1 minute (or warm in a saucepan on the stove top until hot to the touch). Put the warmed milk and cream, egg yolks, sugar, and vanilla into the blender container. Put the lid on securely and turn the dial to the Hot Soup program. Blend until the machine turns itself off (this takes about 5 minutes; steam will rise from the lid when it is finished). Pour the mixture into a bowl and let it come to room temperature, then cover and chill for at least 4 hours or up to 1 day. (To speed up this process, place the bowl of custard over another bowl of ice water and stir with a rubber spatula until chilled.)

To make the ice cream, pour the chilled custard mixture into the blender container. Add the frozen peaches and raspberries. Put the lid on securely and turn the dial to the Frozen Dessert program. Turn the machine on and blend, using the tamper to push the ingredients into the blades, until the machine turns itself off.

Serve right away (the ice cream will be soft) or transfer it to a freezer container, cover, and freeze until firm, up to 4 days.

fresh berries
with warm white-chocolate cream

Cold berries cloaked with warm cream; smooth sauce topped with crisp coconut: It's the contrast of textures and temperatures that makes this dessert unforgettable. Buy top-quality white chocolate in bars and chop it yourself; white chocolate chips will not produce the desired result.

Preheat the oven to 350°F (180°C). Spread the coconut in a pie pan and toast in the oven until golden-brown, stirring once or twice, 8–10 minutes. Alternatively, stir the coconut in a small, nonstick skillet over medium heat until golden brown, about 5 minutes. Let the coconut cool. (Toasted coconut keeps, covered, for several days at room temperature.)

Pour the coconut milk into the blender container and add the white chocolate. Put the lid on securely, turn the variable speed dial to 1, and start the machine. Increase the speed to the highest setting and blend for 3 minutes, until mixture is hot and foamy and the chocolate is melted.

Divide the chilled berries among small bowls. Pour the warm sauce over each portion, sprinkle with the toasted coconut, and serve.

½ cup (2 oz/60 g) shredded coconut

1 cup (8 fl oz/250 ml) unsweetened coconut milk (not light)

7 oz (220 g) good-quality white chocolate (not chips), chopped

2–3 cups (8–12 oz/250–375 g) chilled mixed berries, such as blackberries, blueberries, raspberries and sliced strawberries

Makes 4–6 servings

tiramisu semifreddo

16 chocolate wafers, such as
Nabisco Famous

2 cups (16 fl oz/500 ml)
heavy cream

½ cup (2 oz/60 g)
confectioners' sugar

2 tablespoons strong brewed
coffee or espresso, cooled

2 tablespoons rum or
brandy, optional

1 tablespoon vanilla extract

Pinch of salt

1 lb (500 g) mascarpone
cheese

Makes 12 servings

This semi-frozen dessert is molded in a loaf pan and
served sliced, but for a more casual presentation,
you can layer it in a bowl and scoop out each serving.

Line a 9-by-5-inch (23-by-13-cm) loaf pan with a piece of plastic wrap large enough to line all the sides and drape it over the top. Set aside.

Put the chocolate wafers in the blender container. Put the lid on securely and turn the variable speed dial to 5. Pulse several times until the cookies are finely ground. Transfer the crumbs to a bowl and set aside.

Put the cream, confectioners' sugar, coffee, rum, if using, vanilla, salt, and mascarpone in the blender container (you don't need to rinse it out first). Put the lid on securely, turn the dial to variable speed 1, and start the machine. Increase the speed to the highest setting and blend for 20 seconds, until the mixture is the texture of stiffly whipped cream. (If the mixture is not whipped, pulse it at variable 8 a few times to get the right texture; you will hear a change of sound when it is achieved. Be careful not to overmix. If you do overmix, transfer the mixture to a bowl and whisk in a few tablespoons of cold milk or cream until fluffy.)

Sprinkle the bottom of the lined pan with one-fifth of the crumbs. Spoon in one-fourth of the cream mixture, then gently spread it in an even layer with an offset spatula or the back of a spoon. Sprinkle with another fifth of the crumbs, then smooth another fourth of the cream mixture over the crumb layer. Repeat the layers and sprinkle with a final layer of crumbs. Fold in the edges of the plastic wrap to loosely cover the pan and freeze until the edges start to harden and mixture is firm to the touch, 2–4 hours.

To serve, lift the plastic to remove the semifreddo from the pan. Remove the plastic wrap, then cut the semifreddo crosswise into 12 slices with a sharp knife that has been dipped in warm water. Arrange slices on plates. (You can also freeze the semifreddo for up to 2 days and let stand at room temperature for 15–20 minutes to soften before slicing.)

index

weldonowen

415 Jackson Street, Suite 200, San Francisco, CA 94111
Telephone: 415 291 0100 Fax: 415 291 8841
www.weldonowen.com

Weldon Owen is a division of

BONNIER

WELDON OWEN, INC.

CEO and President Terry Newell
VP, Sales and Marketing Amy Kaneko

Associate Publisher Jennifer Newens

Creative Director Emma Boys
Art Director Ashley Lima

Production Director Chris Hemesath
Associate Production Director Michelle Duggan

Photographer Maren Caruso
Food Stylist Kim Kissling
Prop Stylist Leigh Noe

SMOOTHIES & BEYOND

Conceived and produced by Weldon Owen, Inc.
Copyright © 2014 Weldon Owen, Inc.

This book has been previously published
as *The Art of Blending*

Printed and bound by 1010 Printing, Ltd. in China

First printed in 2014
10 9 8 7 6 5 4 3 2 1

Library of Congress Cataloging-in-Publication
data is available.

ISBN-13: 978-1-61628-803-7
ISBN-10: 1-61628-803-5

ACKNOWLEDGMENTS
Weldon Owen wishes to thank the following people for their generous support
in producing this book: Emily Garland, Sean Franzen, Kim Laidlaw, Kurt Lundquist,
Rachel Lopez Metzger, David Marks, Lex Weibel, and Vita-Mix Corporation.

Vitamix, Professional Series, and 750 are all trademarks of Vita-Mix Corporation.